THE KREGEL PICTORIAL GUIDE TO CHURCH HISTORY

VOLUME 2—THE EARLY CHURCH
A.D. 33–500

JOHN D. HANNAH

kregel
PUBLICATIONS

The Kregel Pictorial Guide to Church History, Volume 2 by John D. Hannah

© 2004 Lion Hudson plc/Tim Dowley & Peter Wyart trading as Three's Company

Text © 2004 Kregel Publications

Published by Kregel Publications, a division of Kregel, Inc, PO Box 2607, Grand Rapids, MI 49501.

Designed by Peter Wyart

Worldwide co-edition produced by Lion Hudson plc,
Mayfield House,
256 Banbury Road, Oxford OX2 7DH, England.
Telephone: +44 (0) 1865 302750.
Fax: +44 (0) 1865 302757.

Email: coed@lionhudson.com.
www.lionhudson.com

Printed in Singapore

Picture acknowledgements

Photographs
The Bridgeman Art Library: pp. 8, 13 top
Tim Dowley: pp.13 bottom, 24, 28
Peter Wyart: p. 31

Maps
Hardlines

Charts
Peter Wyart

Introduction

The beginning of the church was both the climax of an era and the arrival of another. The Age of Anticipation, in which the Hebrew Scriptures progressively disclosed the coming of a great deliverer, ended with the incarnation of Jesus, who is the Christ. A new age dawned; it was a mystery not fully revealed until that time (Eph. 3:1–10). As promised, God turned His mercies toward the inclusion of the Gentiles. Then began a new epoch: the Church Age. What was enfolded or hidden in the Old Testament Scriptures was now unfolded or disclosed. This "new age"—the "last days" (Heb. 1:1–2; 9:10, 26; Acts 3:19–24)—has now stretched over two millennia. Christians gather throughout the world in increasing numbers to reflect on the Lord's first coming as redeemer of His people and anticipate His return as judge of the nations. When the Lord comes again, He will bring an era of fulfillment. Not one of God's promises will fail. Meanwhile, the span between the first and second comings of Christ is the era of the church, the era of the creation of the new people of God.

The history of the Lord's church may be divided into several periods: the Ancient Period (33–500), Medieval Period (500–1500), Early Modern Period (1500–1750), Late Modern Period (1750–1900), and the Postmodern Period (1900–present). Scholars have further divided the time of the church under the Roman Empire, the Ancient Period, into several subdivisions.

John D. Hannah

Contents

The Dawning of a New Era (33–100)

The Old Testament Scriptures end with a promise that "Elijah" would come and inaugurate a new era (Mal. 4:5). This prophecy was realized in John the Baptizer (Luke 1:17), who announced the Messiah (John 1:19–30). The age of promises had ended and a new age had dawned.

The Setting of the Church

Christ came into this world in the "fullness of time" (Gal. 4:4), a time period that was unique. God had providentially orchestrated the stage of history—its cast of characters and circumstances—for the coming of His Son and the beginning of His church. Politically, the iron arm of Roman strength was everywhere felt in the region of the Mediterranean. The Roman world was one of law with a measure of peace. The Romans permitted unhindered travel, offered military protection, and repressed piracy (Acts 16:37; 22:25). A vast road system across the empire served military purposes, but it also gave the apostles ease of travel. A military system often known for its cruel repression also brought the gospel to the very edges of the empire. Though Roman legions conquered Greece, the influence of the Greek culture was pivotal. Greek was the trade language of the empire until it was replaced by Latin in the third century. Using this common tongue, the gospel was able to penetrate anywhere in the Roman Empire.

Christianity's Jewish roots also greatly buttressed the birth and expansion of the church. In Jesus' day, there was a great expectancy for Israel's deliverer, the Christ or Messiah (Luke 1:25–34). The nation felt it was on the edge of a new era, and that Roman oppression would soon end. The scattering of the Jews throughout the Roman world and the creation of the synagogue system were vital to the spread of the church. The apostle Paul's missionary strategy was to travel to cities with Jewish concentrations, and he turned to the Gentiles only after being repulsed by the Jews (Acts 13:14; 14:1; 17:1, 17; 18:4, 19; 19:8).

The Coming of Christ

The apostle John encapsulated the meaning of the advent of Christ succinctly when he said, "The Word became flesh and dwelt among us" (John 1:14). Though He was eternal God—robed with splendor and majesty—the Son humbled Himself in identifying with humanity and, as the God/Man, taking the lowly position of a servant (Phil. 2:6–8). In His life, Jesus Christ fulfilled the righteousness of the law, which Adam had failed to do when he plunged the race into destruction and death. Christ, the Son of God, in His death on the cross, liberated the race by taking upon Himself the sin of the world and suffering its horrible consequences: punishment and death. Therefore God, who forever is holy and just, could grant grace and righteousness to those who are in Christ. Jesus perfectly paid sin's debt, and so God is perfectly just in freeing believers from its penalty (Rom. 3:26). The proof of this seemingly incredible mercy is Jesus' resurrection. Because He satisfied God completely with regard to sin, death could no longer have mastery over Him or His people; death in fact has been banished. Simeon summarized the ministry of Christ when he held the child Jesus in his arms. "A light to bring salvation to the Gentiles and the glory of your people Israel" (Luke 2:32).

The Birth of the Church

Two millennia before the coming of Christ, God promised Abraham that He would make of him a great nation (Gen. 12:2; Gal. 3:7–8). Through Jesus Christ, the true son of Abraham (Gal. 3:16), salvation has come to all people (Gal. 3:28). The mystery of the new people of God promised in the Hebrew Scriptures (Jer. 31:31–34; Heb. 8:7–13) is fulfilled in the church (Eph. 3:1–11; Rom. 11:17–24), in which Gentiles have been made fellow heirs with Jews in the body of Christ.

Jesus promised His disciples that He would not leave them without a comforting guide, but that He would send them another like Himself (John 14:26–31; 15:26). They were instructed to wait in Jerusalem for the Holy Spirit (Acts 1:4). In the events recorded in Acts 2, the Spirit came to indwell His people and the Age of the Spirit began. The church—a people gathered from the nations who recognized Jesus as "Lord and Christ" (Acts 2:36)—came into existence.

The Expansion of the Church

The church grew rapidly from the Day of Pentecost (the Feast of Firstfruits), as thousands embraced faith in Christ. Through the diversity of people who gathered for Israel's great feast, the good news was scattered across the world. The first gathering places were homes in various cities and the temple complex in Jerusalem, where the new believers "continued steadfastly in the apostles' teachings and fellowship, breaking of bread, and in prayers" (Acts 2:42; see also 5:42). The focus of the apostles' preaching was the person and work of Jesus Christ, His death and resurrection.

The book of Acts provides a limited, yet extremely important, history of the church in the first century. The focus of Luke's account is the spread of the gospel through the apostles, primarily Paul, toward the capital of the empire, Rome. Not only does Luke want his readers to know the message of the church from the lips of its earliest leaders, but he also introduces them to the power of the gospel. Its message triumphs over every difficulty and expression of paganism in its path. Within thirty years, the message of Christ was firmly planted throughout the Roman empire.

The gospel was originally described as "The Way," and followers of Christ were first known as "Christians" in the city of Antioch (Acts 11:26). In the early second century, this movement became known as "Christianity," for it was composed of those who followed the Christ, or Messiah. The message of forgiveness through Christ transformed many lives, filling believers with a new sense of identity, mission, and cultural compassion. Other people, however, reacted with rage against the new movement and Christians experienced ridicule, persecution, and even martyrdom. Adversity, however, seemed to steel the resolve of Christ's people to share the good news even more.

The church was composed of Jews, former proselytes to Judaism (called God-fearers) who attended the synagogues, and Gentiles. Many were from the lower castes of society; many were slaves or former slaves. There were some exceptions, but Paul describes the early believers as "not many wise according to the flesh, not many mighty, not many noble . . . God has chosen the foolish things of the world to confound the wise" (1 Cor. 1:26–27).

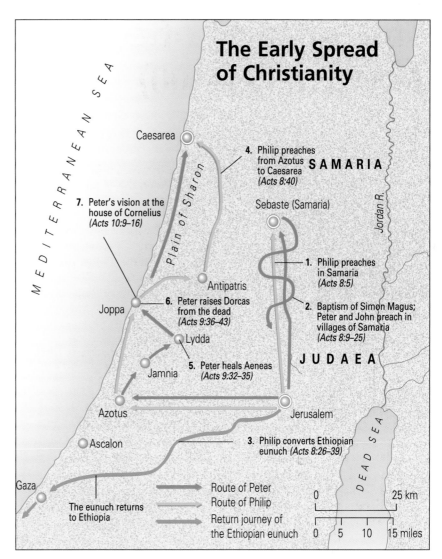

The Early Spread of Christianity

4. Philip preaches from Azotus to Caesarea (*Acts 8:40*)

7. Peter's vision at the house of Cornelius (*Acts 10:9–16*)

1. Philip preaches in Samaria (*Acts 8:5*)

2. Baptism of Simon Magus; Peter and John preach in villages of Samaria (*Acts 8:9–25*)

6. Peter raises Dorcas from the dead (*Acts 9:36–43*)

5. Peter heals Aeneas (*Acts 9:32–35*)

3. Philip converts Ethiopian eunuch (*Acts 8:26–39*)

Caesarea · SAMARIA · Sebaste (Samaria) · Antipatris · Joppa · Lydda · Jamnia · Azotus · Ascalon · Gaza · JUDAEA · Jerusalem

MEDITERRANEAN SEA · Plain of Sharon · Jordan R. · DEAD SEA

The eunuch returns to Ethiopia

Route of Peter
Route of Philip
Return journey of the Ethiopian eunuch

0   25 km
0   5   10   15 miles

The Organization of the Church

The earliest gatherings of Christians were marked by simplicity in structure and form. James, the brother of Jesus, appears to have had a role of leadership with the apostles and elders in Jerusalem (Acts 15:2), though at the so-called Jerusalem Council the "whole church" gave their consent (Acts 15:22). From the later writings of Paul, we learn that there were four offices in the church as a whole: apostles, prophets, evangelists, and pastor/teachers (Eph. 4:11). The first three offices seem to have been designed to serve all the churches by means of traveling itinerants, such as the apostle Paul. The office of pastor/teacher served

a local gathering of saints.

Within the local house churches (Rom. 16:5, 14–15), leadership resided in several recognized offices. First, each local church had elders, also called bishops (originally these were interchangeable terms. See Titus 1:5, 7; Acts 20:17, 28). Elders appear first in the list of officers (Phil. 1:1; 1 Tim. 3), always in plurality (Acts 20:17; Heb. 13:7), and form a group called a presbytery (1 Tim. 4:14). There were also deacons that assisted the elders, overseeing the duties of service. It seems that there was a guarded independence among the churches; there is clearly no indication of the hierarchical government structures over local churches that would emerge centuries later.

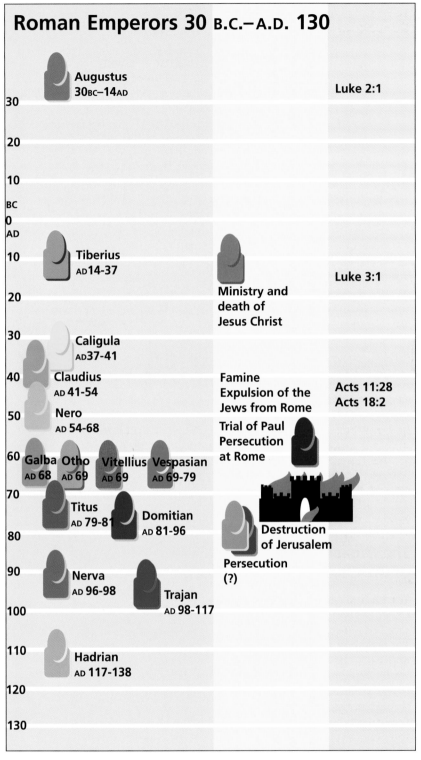

Roman Emperors 30 B.C.–A.D. 130

Augustus 30BC–14AD	Luke 2:1
Tiberius AD 14-37	Luke 3:1
	Ministry and death of Jesus Christ
Caligula AD 37-41	
Claudius AD 41-54	Famine Expulsion of the Jews from Rome — Acts 11:28 Acts 18:2
Nero AD 54-68	Trial of Paul Persecution at Rome
Galba AD 68 Otho AD 69 Vitellius AD 69 Vespasian AD 69-79	
Titus AD 79-81 Domitian AD 81-96	Destruction of Jerusalem
Nerva AD 96-98 Trajan AD 98-117	Persecution (?)
Hadrian AD 117-138	

Timeline markings: 30, 20, 10, BC, 0, AD, 10, 20, 30, 40, 50, 60, 70, 80, 90, 100, 110, 120, 130

The Worship of the Church

It early became the custom of the believers to gather on Sundays, the day of new beginnings. From the information available from the Bible, Christians gathered to participate together in the worship of God. The gifts of the Spirit such as prophecy, tongues, and words of knowledge were regularly practiced to edify the faithful. Itinerant apostles, prophets, and evangelists supplemented the teaching and guiding ministry of the local leadership. From Paul's writings we can surmise that the gatherings were at times tragically unruly, even chaotic (1 Cor. 11:30). Apparently, the meetings were not exclusively for Christians (1 Cor. 14:23). The nature of the participation of women in these gatherings is disputed, but it seems clear that they prayed and prophesied. They were prohibited from publicly challenging a teacher or a teaching. The emphasis in the churches was on the unity of the faith and mutual interdependence of believers, not the marked individualism that characterizes the Postmodern Period.

The churches were devoid of many modern complexities. There were no saints' days or elaborate feasts. The only annual celebration seems to have been of the Resurrection. Two sacraments or "divine mysteries" were celebrated: the Eucharist or Lord's Supper, and baptism—though some churches would claim that there were more. The earliest Christian documents do not afford us an undisputed interpretation of the ordinances. The Eucharist appears to have been observed at every gathering of the church for worship (1 Cor. 11:20), and may have occurred around a communal meal (Luke 22:20). Baptism was seen as the entrance into the church, the redeemed community; in later centuries it became quite distorted in its definition.

The elements of worship included "reading, exhortation, and the teaching of doctrine" (1 Tim. 4:13). The Hebrew Scriptures were read, as was correspondence from the apostles. Prayer was also a crucial element of worship. Without a professional class of clergy or buildings to maintain, the financial burdens were low; however, the New Testament records that Christians gave to Paul and to the poor in Jerusalem.

The Earliest Fathers (100–150)

The Fathers and the Writings

Though the term "church father" is often used to refer to any writer of the Ancient Period, it is used here in a narrower sense to designate those writers or writings that immediately followed the original apostles, perhaps overlapping somewhat with them. The literary quality of these writings marks them out as unique from later works. These earliest non-canonical writings are pastoral in tone; they are concerned with the conduct and management of the churches; and devoid of the combativeness that would come to characterize the writings of the late second century.

The writings of the earliest Fathers are few in number. Most come from the eastern Mediterranean, where the church emerged. (This is not an argument that the Orthodox Church is the earliest and original church, because the early church and the Orthodox Church differ in many important ways.) Prominent among the churchmen were Ignatius of Antioch, who appears to have coined the term *catholic* to describe the churches in his *Letter to the Smyrnaeans*; Polycarp, bishop of Smyrna and a disciple of the apostle John; and Papias. In the western region of the Mediterranean, Clement of Rome wrote a very important letter to the Corinthians and Hermas, also of Rome, wrote a much-appreciated allegory titled *The Shepherd*. Among the writings without a known author are *The Homily of Clement*—an early sermon—and the *Didache*, a manual of church practice.

The Fathers and Authority

Christianity emerged as an extension of its rich roots in Judaism. As such, many parallels exist between the two. Indeed, Christians such as Justin Martyr argued very early that Christian faith is the fulfillment of Jewish faith. The Jewish feasts—such as the Passover, the Feast of Firstfruits, and the Day of Atonement—prefigure the person and work of Jesus Christ. The earliest organization of the church suggests roots in the Sanhedrin. This is most clearly seen in the dependence of the early church upon the Hebrew Scriptures as its authority. The writings of the apostles were revered, but the notion of these documents being of equal importance to the Hebrew Scriptures was not grasped. Some of the earliest writings of the Fathers were highly esteemed in the churches, such as the *Didache*, *The Shepherd of Hermas*, and Clement's *Letter to the Corinthians*.

On the authority of the gospel—which for the most part was orally based rather than textual (the word *martyr* means "witness")—

The Apostolic Fathers

Name	Dates	Where They Served	Works	Important Facts
Clement of Rome	c. 30–c. 100	Rome	I Clement	Perhaps mentioned in Phil. 4:3 Martyred under Domitian
Ignatius	d. 117	Antioch in Syria	To the Ephesians To the Magnesians To the Romans To the Philadelphians To the Smyrnaeans	Opposed Gnostic heresies Martyred under Trajan
Hermas	late 1st to early 2nd century	Rome	The Shepherd (an allegory)	Contemporary of Clement Perhaps a former Jewish slave
Papias	c. 60–c. 130	Hierapolis	Exposition of the Oracles of Our Lord	Acquaintance of the apostle John Held premillennial views Claimed Mark's Gospel was based on Peter's words
Polycarp	c. 69–160	Smyrna	Epistle to the Philippians	Acquaintance of the apostle John Martyred under Antoninus Pius

the church argued for the apostolic succession of the truth. Churchmen, such as Clement, declared that their message was true because it came from an apostle, who received it from direct communication with Christ, who came from God. It was important for leaders in the churches to identify with an apostle, because that assured the trustworthiness of their message. From this defense of the Christian faith came the need for each church to be able to trace its genealogical origins back to an apostle through its leadership. This was the root of a later doctrine of apostolic succession; it was a way to preserve and communicate the truth.

The Fathers, Christ, and Salvation

If the earliest churchmen viewed their faith from a corporate rather than an individual perspective, they were neither speculative nor rationalistic in it. It was not until centuries later that the church felt compelled to express its beliefs in such a manner. It was enough for believers to speak of Christ as "the Lord of the entire universe" and as "our God." The writer of *The Homily of Clement* (sometimes called *II Clement*) asked his readers "to think of Jesus as of God, as the judge of the living and the dead." Christ was God incarnate, through whom salvation came to His people by His sacrifice. Clement of Rome stated, "Let us fix our gaze on the blood of Christ, because it was poured out for our salvation and brought the grace of repentance to the whole world." It is not too much to assert that the early church was Christ-centered.

The Fathers and Church Government

Within the authority structure of the churches, a remarkable

Wall painting of eucharistic meal from the third century catacombs of Priscilla, Rome.

transition took place with the rise of the bishop's office: the leadership of individual churches gradually passed from a plurality and parity of leaders to a singular leader. The *Didache* speaks of a plurality of leaders who are chosen from the congregation, as does Hermas of Rome. However, Ignatius of Antioch explains that each church should have one bishop and two other offices: elder and deacon. Perhaps for the better defense of the faith, he instructs his hearers to "do nothing without the bishop." The test of orthodoxy was conformity to the bishop, because the office of bishop came from God. Further, it seems that bishops were chosen by and from the congregation throughout the Ancient Period.

The combination of Clement of Rome's idea of the apostolic succession of the truth and Ignatius's concept of a single bishop over each church shifted the government of the churches to a quasi-episcopal form. These

trends would predominate in the churches by the late second century.

The Fathers and the Sacraments

The churches appear to have embraced two sacraments or ordinances: baptism and the Eucharist, or Lord's Supper. Although baptism was more fully explained by later writers, in the early years it was universally seen as the means of entrance into the church—thus, into spiritual life (Acts 2:38; 22:16; Titus 3:5). Baptism was to be preceded by a time of fasting. Most baptisms occurred at the celebration of Christ's resurrection. (This seems to be the origin of later Lenten traditions.) It is clear that one came to the water believing he or she would receive the thing signified by the water: an inward cleansing. The manner of baptism does not appear to be an issue; it

Background: Coin of the Roman emperor Hadrian.

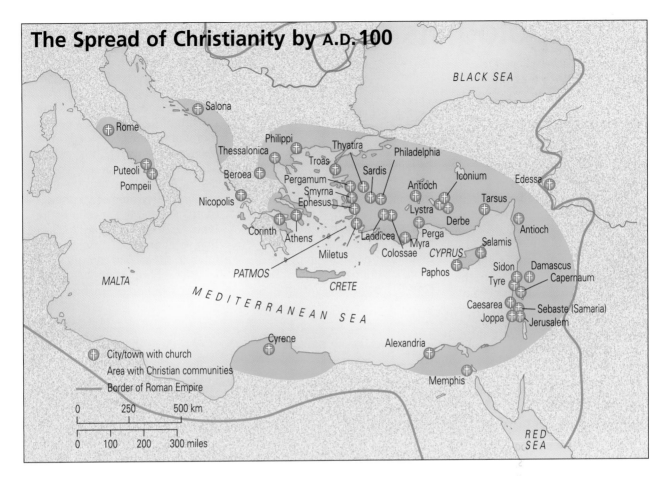

The Spread of Christianity by A.D. 100

BLACK SEA

Salona
Rome
Philippi
Thessalonica
Troas
Thyatira
Philadelphia
Puteoli
Pompeii
Beroea
Pergamum
Sardis
Iconium
Edessa
Nicopolis
Smyrna
Antioch
Tarsus
Ephesus
Lystra
Corinth
Athens
Laodicea
Derbe
Perga
Antioch
Miletus
Colossae
Myra
Salamis
PATMOS
CYPRUS
Sidon
Damascus
MALTA
Paphos
Tyre
Capernaum
Caesarea
Sebaste (Samaria)
Joppa
Jerusalem
Cyrene
Alexandria
Memphis
CRETE
MEDITERRANEAN SEA
RED SEA

✛ City/town with church
Area with Christian communities
— Border of Roman Empire

0   250   500 km
0 100 200 300 miles

Polycarp (c. 69–c. 155) was martyred in Rome at the age of 86.

could be by immersion or by pouring, using warm or cold water.

Just as baptism was the symbol of entrance into life, so the Lord's Supper was the symbol of fellowship in that life. (Life and the gathering of the saints was intricately interconnected.) The early church did not think in terms of individuality, but as a corporate body. The group met to celebrate together the new life in the Savior at a common table with common elements. The meal was seen as a thanksgiving celebration of Christ's life and death for the community (the meaning of the term *Eucharist*). Christ was truly present at the table, though the manner in which He was present was not a subject of thoughtful consideration.

The Fathers and "Last Things"

The earliest writers after the apostles embraced three central ideas about future events: the coming of Christ, imminently and visibly; the resurrection of believers and unbelievers; and the destruction of the present world followed by the kingdom of God. There is little uniformity among them in details. They envisioned a coming kingdom, but they cannot be classified as embracing the idea of a thousand-year reign of Christ on earth. It is perhaps best to call them "quasi-premillennarians." The purpose of the kingdom was viewed in a variety of ways: a period of rest for believers, a worldwide reign by Christ, an era of the triumph of Christians, or the future home for believers. There seems to have been an unwillingness to sharply separate the kingdom from the eternal state. The earliest Christians were filled with hope and joy.

The Apologists (150–300)

As the church emerged as an increasingly potent force in the Roman empire, critics became progressively more strident, often destructively so. Christian truth–claims came under attack from adversaries, necessitating a response. In answering their critics, churchmen began to formulate the church's teachings in an orderly fashion. Because of the polemical tone of their writings, these bishops have been called *apologists*.

The Apologists and the Roman State

Christians were not welcomed in the empire, because they posed a threat to the flourishing polytheistic religions of the time. To confess faith in only one God was regarded as little more than atheism. Further, the later emperors were often accorded divine honors, yet it was unfathomable for Christians to worship anyone but King Jesus. Many felt that the Christians' neglect of the gods would incur the gods' wrath. As a result, Christians were often blamed for natural and political disasters. An African proverb asserted, "If God does not send rain, they blame it on the Christians." In order to discredit them, Christians were charged with moral offenses such as incest and killing children in order to consume their blood in the Eucharist.

Persecution
Consequently, the church often felt the wrath of the state through persecution; many sealed their devotion to Christ with their lives.

Tertullian commented, "The blood of the martyrs is the seed of the church." The more the church suffered, the more it grew. Two eras were particularly tragic because of the empire-wide calamitous persecution of the church. During the reign of Decius (249–51), coinciding with the millennial anniversary of Rome, Christians were blamed for the decline of the empire. The last widespread persecution came during the reign of Diocletian (303–11). However, each of these periods of suffering was a defining moment for the church. For many believers, following Christ meant accepting mockery and often death. The Bible records the first-century martyrdom of Stephen (Acts 7:60) and the apostle James (Acts 12:2). Later writings indicate that Peter and Paul suffered similar fates. In the second century, Ignatius, bishop of Antioch, and Polycarp, bishop of Smyrna, were

martyred. From the third century, there is the record of Perpetua, a mother, and five friends who were put to death. Later, the church came to pay such honor to the martyrs that their remains and relics were made objects of veneration and intercession.

Lapsed Christians

The more general persecutions of the middle third and early fourth centuries caused a serious dispute in the church because some renounced their Christian profession to avoid persecution and then later wanted to be readmitted to the church. This issue raised the important question of the nature of the church: Is membership in God's church to be defined by costly discipleship and holiness, or by its redemptive nature? If the former view is correct, the lapsed ones should not be readmitted; but if the latter view is correct, readmission is a necessity because there is no salvation outside the church.

Is the church defined by its moral standards or by grace? Cyprian argued in the middle of the third century that the church is defined as grace-imparting, that there is only one church, and traditors (those who had lapsed under the pressure of persecution) should be granted full membership after they repented. The followers of Novatus, the Novatians, argued that in admitting the lapsed, the church became apostate, and therefore no longer had a claim to being the true church. When the same issues reemerged in the fourth century, Augustine championed Cyprian's position with even greater tenacity against the Donatists.

A second question dealt with the spiritual benefit of sacraments performed by one who had faltered in persecution. Does the spiritual integrity of the priest determine the spiritual benefit of his office? Cyprian and Augustine argued that it does not. These controversies defined the church in light of its grace-providing function, buttressing the idea that salvation is only in the historic church, the one that can trace its genealogy to the apostles.

The Apologists and the Heresies

Gnosticism

The threat of false teachings came both from outside the church and from within. The most potent outside threat was Gnosticism (from the word *gnosis,* meaning "knowledge"), which incorporated elements of Christian faith and pagan thought. Though not uniform in their teachings, the Gnostics argued that a basic dualism defines the world: spirit and matter. All things material are evil; the spiritual realm alone is true. Mankind is a spirit trapped in the limitations of the material, the source of all problems. The world was not created by God, but by a semi-god (a partly material super being). Redemption, according to the Gnostics, came by living above the material world and the way of doing so was revealed by Christ. They asserted that Christ did not have a physical body, but only appeared to and He did not die on

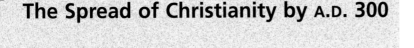

The Spread of Christianity by A.D. 300

PANNONIA

DACIA

DALMATIA

MOESIA

THRACIA

MACEDONIA

EPIRUS

ACHAIA

CRETA

Danube R.

BLACK SEA

BITHYNIA AND PONTUS

Byzantium

GALATIA

CAPPADOCIA

ASIA

LYCIA AND PAMPHYLIA

CILICIA

Euphrates R.

ARMENIA

MESOPOTAMIA

Antioch

SYRIA

CYPRUS

M E D I T E R R A N E A N S E A

JUDAEA

Alexandria

CYRENAICA

AEGYPTUS

Roman Persecutions of Christians

Date	Emperor	Scope of Persecution	Important Martyrs
64	Nero	In and around Rome Christians made scapegoats for fire of Rome	Paul Peter
c. 90–96	Domitian	In Rome and Asia Minor Christians persecuted for refusing "emperor worship"	Clement of Rome John (exiled to Patmos)
98–117	Trajan	Sporadically enforced Christians executed when found but not sought out	Ignatius Rufus
117–138	Hadrian	Sporadic	
161–180	Marcus Aurelius	Emperor was a Stoic who opposed Christianity on philosophical grounds	Justin Martyr Blandina
202–211	Septimus Severus	Conversion to Christianity forbidden	Irenaeus Perpetua
235–236	Maximinus the Thracian	Christian clergy executed	Ursula Hippolytus
249–251	Decius	First empire-wide persecution Enthusiastic return to paganism	Fabianus Alexander of Jerusalem
257–260	Valerian	Christians' property confiscated Christians prohibited right of assembly	Origen Cyprian
303–311	Diocletian Galerius	The worst persecution Churches destroyed, Bibles burned All civil rights of Christians suspended	Alban

a cross to purchase salvation.

Two additional heresies, Neoplatonism and Manichaeism, had an impact on the church, both teaching a cosmic dualism (material is disparaged) and salvation by means of asceticism (self-denial, self-effort). Manichaeism, based on the teaching of Mani, deeply influenced Augustine before his Christian conversion. These false teachings caused churchmen to reflect on the issues of authority, Christ as truly human (the Creator and the Redeemer as one and the same), and the creation as good though corrupted.

Ebionites

False teachers emerged from within the churches, as well, rending and weakening it. Ebionites, followers of Ebion, struggled with the important question of the relationship of the Old Testament law to the Christian faith, the connection of the Hebrew Scriptures to the church. Ebionites taught that Paul had twisted the truth by neglecting the rightful place of the law, and overemphasizing faith. Often they denied the deity of Jesus Christ and taught obedience to the law for salvation.

Marcionites

Another group that proved heretical, yet sought to describe the relation of the Hebrew Scriptures to the church, was the Marcionites. The followers of Marcion argued that Christianity had no connection at all to the law, that they are antithetical ways of salvation (quite the opposite of the Ebionites). Marcion saw the God of the Old Testament as a distinct and inferior God to the God of the newer writings. He rejected the Hebrew Scriptures that described a wrathful, judgmental deity, as well as newer writings that seem influenced by those Scriptures. He disparaged Matthew, Mark, Acts, and Hebrews; eliminated what he saw as spurious materials from other books; and saw only a portion of Paul's epistles as genuine. The rejection of Marcion's teachings—though his influence would be felt for two centuries—caused the church to think about the relationship of the Hebrew Scriptures to the Greek Scriptures, the Old Testament to the New. Immediately, the bishops saw continuity, not discontinuity in the writings. They understood that the Old Testament anticipates the New; the New Testament completes the "book of shadows," the Old Testament.

Montanists

The Montanists were a second-century restoration or primitive movement. They argued that the church had grown lax morally, that the role of the laity had declined with the growing power of bishops, and that spiritual gifts had been neglected. Some among the Montanists stressed the prophetic, authoritative gifts and the continuation of divine revelation. They frequently promoted

Artist's impression of the martyrdom of Christians in the Roman Colosseum.

uncontrolled emotional extremes. The rejection of the movement, though its most influential proponent was the great Tertullian, forced the church to examine the issue of authority and the canon of Scripture.

The Apologists and Their Contributions

In contending for the faith in response to heresy, the apologists—the earliest bishops in the church—began to construct a Christian theology. The majority of them were from the eastern Mediterranean region, though a few were from the West. It would not be accurate to describe them as theologians in the modern sense of the term; but they answered their critics, defended Christian truth, and explained the Christian faith.

Justin Martyr
Justin Martyr (c. 100–c. 165) wrote an apologetic to Trypho, a Jew, in which he argued that fulfilled prophecy proved that Jesus was the promised Christ of the Hebrew Scriptures. A true Old Testament Israelite, he said, is now a Christian. In his *First Apology*, Justin argued that whatever truth was found in philosophy came from Moses and the indwelling presence of God in every man. A true philosopher, therefore, like a true Jew, is now a follower of Christ. Justin sought to explain the relationship of Christ to God, which is the center of Christian witness.

Irenaeus
Among the early apologists, Irenaeus's (c. 140–202) contribution makes him the greatest churchman prior to the fourth century, when Athanasius came on the scene. A prolific writer and the bishop of Lyon in the West, Irenaeus defended the truth claims of the faith by arguing that Scripture (the written gospel) and tradition (the oral message of the apostles) were of equal authority in the churches (1 Tim. 6:20–21; 2 Tim. 1:13–14; 2:2). He connected tradition with apostolic succession, suggesting— as had Clement of Rome before him—that God had given His message to Christ, Christ had

The remains of the Roman Colosseum today.

Justin Martyr (c. 100–c. 165).

Tertullian (c. 155–c. 240).

Irenaeus (c. 140–202)

passed the message down to the apostles, and the apostles had passed the message of God along to the bishops. It was important, therefore, that each church demonstrate the genealogical connection of its bishops to the apostles, because, Irenaeus contended, that connection proved the truthfulness of the gospel message. Among the churches with apostolic connection, he argued that the Roman bishop was superior to the others, because the Roman church had been founded by two apostles, Peter and Paul, an insight that came to be abused in later centuries.

In *Against Heresies*, Irenaeus spoke against the error of the Gnostics, arguing that the Hebrew and Greek Scriptures were not opposed to each other, rather, they have a complementary theme throughout: redemption through the Messiah. He argued that God is one; the creator of the spiritual and the material is the giver of the incarnate Son, Jesus Christ. Christ had a true humanity as well as being truly God. Also, Irenaeus argued that Adam lost life for all humanity through his disobedience, but that Christ restores life through the redeeming mercies of His own grace and life.

Tertullian

Tertullian (c. 155–c. 240), a North African churchman, wrote on a wide variety of subjects. Though his contribution was enormous, immediate appreciation of his efforts was clouded by his departure from the church to join the Montanists. Writing in Latin, he coined numerous terms that have come into the church's vocabulary. For example, he coined the terms *trinity* (threeness), *person* (within plurality is a singularity), and *substance* (the essence of the commonality). He is also known for his strident antagonism toward philosophy: "What has Jerusalem to do with Athens . . . [or] the church with the academy?" He opposed philosophy as a source of truth that rivaled God's revelation, but not as a method of argumentation. Like Irenaeus, Tertullian wrote against Marcion's followers and the Gnostics, arguing that the Hebrew Scriptures and Greek writings are the one revelation of God.

Cyprian

Cyprian (c. 205–258), a North African bishop and martyr, wrote in the context of severe persecution and the spread of heterodoxy. He was concerned with those who lapsed from the

faith in troublesome times. Should believers who had renounced the faith be allowed back into the church? Cyprian argued that they should be rebaptized and readmitted because of the redeeming nature of the church. The church is the ark of salvation and there is no salvation outside of it. So, to deny readmission would be to deny sinners the place where the gospel of Christ is to be found and the grace of God dispensed. Also, Cyprian contended, there is only one apostolic and catholic church. "He who does not have the church for his mother cannot have God for his father." To join any other group is to be outside the true gospel. He believed that Rome had priority among the bishops throughout the empire, because of Peter and Paul. However, he also believed that all the bishops were equal in authority, that not even the bishop of Rome had the right to meddle in the affairs of other churches. (At this time, there was no hierarchy over all the churches, simply a confederation of equals throughout the empire.)

Origen

One of the more accomplished interpreters of Scripture during this period was Origen of Alexandria,

Some early Christian symbols (*left to right*): The Good Shepherd; the anchor, incorporating the cross; and the dove.

Egypt (c. 185–c. 253). While Origen affirmed the truthfulness of Scripture, he approached the Bible with a multi-level perspective (literal, moral, and spiritual). The deepest meaning of the Bible is not in the literal text, he said, but is often in the spiritualized or allegorical text, a meaning *under* the words. With this view of the Bible, Origen sought to defend it from critics like Celsus, discover its profoundest treasures, and deepen the church's moral and devotional life.

Origen's understanding of the Trinity, however, is suspect. He taught that, though both are divine, the Son and the Spirit are inferior to the Father. Further, he seemed to stress the freedom of the will to such an extent that grace seems no longer to be grace. He qualified grace saying, "Our perfection is accomplished neither by our doing nothing, nor yet is it completed by us, but God does the greater part of it." His dependence on Platonic idealism allowed his theology to be detached from Scripture so that he was frequently condemned in the subsequent history of the church for his notion of an eternal creation, preexistence of souls, distortion concerning Christ's sacrifice (taking a "ransom to Satan" view), and for showing hues of universalism.

Significant Theological Developments by the Apologists

The church's understanding of what the Scriptures teach has always been contextual or related to circumstances. Context has provided a lens through which the church answered scriptural questions. As a result, a development of the church's teachings, an emergent self-understanding, is evident in the apologists. In this era when the church was particularly threatened by persecution and theological heresies, these developments for the defense and edification of the body of Christ are noteworthy.

1. The church found a defense of the gospel in the development of the office of bishop. Not only was there a shift from plurality of leadership in the churches by the middle of the second century, but the teaching of apostolic succession emerged through the bishops. The Christian teachings were validated, because each church could demonstrate an unbroken line of succession of leaders back to an apostle of Christ. At that time, all the bishops throughout the empire were considered equal in status and power; no one claimed that one particular bishop was superior to the others.

2. To ensure orthodoxy in its membership, the church developed creedal confessions for use in the baptismal rites. Members were required to confess the Christian faith publicly by answering a series of questions before admission to the church would be recognized. The earliest of these confessions, the Roman Symbol, developed into the Apostle's Creed.

3. In the struggle against heretics, and perhaps because the Marcionites claimed authority for their views from a very restricted portion of Scriptures, churchmen saw the necessity of codifying the sources of the church's teachings. The followers of Marcion rejected the entirety of the Hebrew Scriptures, as well as parts of the apostles' writings. They did not see the unity of the two Testaments.

The Canon of Scripture
From the beginning, the church embraced the Hebrew Scriptures as authoritative; by the late second century, newer writings were also recognized, such as the Gospels and letters of the apostles. Although the idea of an authoritative list of writings emerged early, the exact number of books in the canon was not resolved for centuries.

The earliest list of books to be used in the churches to the exclusion of others is the Muratorian Canon. It refers to only two epistles of John and one of Peter, though it makes the point that some of the churches did not accept the Peter letter as authentic. Eusebius (c. 263–340), the church's first historian, assembled a list used in the churches of his day and found that some did not recognize the Book of Hebrews or the Revelation of John.

At the Council of Laodicea (363), the church issued a canonical list of writings that included Baruch in the Hebrew writings and deleted Revelation from the Greek writings. The Easter Letter of Athanasius (366–67), the bishop of Alexandria, contained Baruch and rejected Esther as canonical. It did, however, include all the New Testament books. Damascus I, bishop of Rome (382), suggested a list that included the Wisdom of Solomon, Ecclesiasticus, Judith, and the two Maccabees in the Old Testament. In the New Testament, he recognized one epistle from John, one from another John, but not a third. Augustine (354–430), the most influential early churchman, believed that the book of Maccabees was canonical.

The Apologists and Church Life

The experience of the earliest Christians was far more church-centered than in modern times. The Christian faith was not viewed as a private experience that improved one's present life and infused it with hope. Faith was a corporate phenomenon expressed in community. (The ancient world was not one that struggled with rampant individualism, privatized pragmatism, and the rationalistic emptiness that characterizes postmodern culture.) The emphasis of the early Christians was that of humbly following Jesus (even if it entailed adverse consequences, including death) and submission to leadership in the churches. Obedience to church leaders secured the unity of the church

and the preservation of correct teaching. The church was viewed as the ark of salvation: to be saved, one had to be a member of it through baptism, and live in compliance with its leaders, the bishops. It was a joyous community, filled with singing and prayer, and with listening and sharing.

Baptism

There were two special signs of grace in the churches: baptism, a symbol of entrance into the community; and the Eucharist or Lord's table, a sign of fellowship in the community of faith. Baptism was seen as the entrance into spiritual life, a view derived from several passages of Scripture (Mark 16:16; John 3:5; Acts 2:38, 22:16; Titus 3:5). Water baptism and life from death were seen as a unity, occurring together, not separate from each other. However, this early concept must be explained carefully. Unlike the modern church, the ancient body of believers saw redemption through community, not individuality. They embraced the need for conversion and commitment, but not instantaneously on demand. It was an educational model of conversion, not a decisional model. Those who were interested in the Christian faith first became disciples or learners (catechumens) for up to three years. They progressed through stages: *weepers* (instructed privately by a Christian but not allowed to worship with the believers), *hearers* (allowed to hear preaching, but not allowed to pray with the church), and *kneelers* (allowed to stay after the preaching for prayers). This was a three-year process. Then, at the annual celebration of the Resurrection of Christ, the catechumens would be instructed by their bishop, fast (the tradition of Lent), and be baptized. They came, believing in Christ, to confess Him in the water, knowing that as surely as they were

Baptism illustrated in a third century wallpainting from a Roman catacomb.

outwardly cleansed by water, they were inwardly cleansed by the Spirit. In this sense, water and salvation were connected. Evidence for the baptism of those incapable of instruction (infants) is not available in the early centuries; the baptized were those who came believing to receive what water signified.

The Eucharist

After baptism, the person was viewed as part of the redeemed community, which allowed them into the fellowship of the saints, mostly graphically symbolized by the Eucharist. The Lord's Table was the center of the worship of the church, a rehearsal of the gospel in symbol (John 6). The presence of Christ in the table celebration was viewed as a real, corporal presence. However, the church did not speculate on the nature of His presence. The grace bestowed through the Eucharist was not redemptive; it was a sanctifying grace. Excommunication meant a separation from the Lord's Supper, the symbol of spiritual life. It was such a serious thing that only repentance, symbolized through penance and contrition, could bring restoration.

The Triumph of the Church in the Empire (300–500)

Constantine the Great

The fortunes of the church in the empire changed unexpectedly in the fourth century. In 312, Constantine, emperor of Gaul (France) and Britain, defeated Maxentius to expand his rule throughout the West. Emboldened by a vision of a cross in the sky, he believed his victory came from the Christian God. Under this first pro-Christian Roman emperor, Christianity was tolerated by the state, thus ending the era of persecution. Constantine's mother, St. Helen, became a zealot for her faith, traveling to the Holy Land to recover the sites of Christ and the early church. The emperor built a second capital in the eastern portion of the empire and named it Constantinople after himself. During the reign of Theodosius I, later in the century, paganism was officially banned and Christianity gained the status of a state religion. Pagan temples were abandoned or turned into centers of Christian worship; scandalous festivals were redefined with a Christian perspective. The church now spread from the Atlantic Ocean to western Asia, from Britain to Africa north of the Sahara Desert. An unprecedented era of church dominance was about to begin.

Powerful Bishops

This era was remarkable, even though not all of the changes that occurred in the fourth century were supportive of a healthy church—for example, the blurring of the separate duties of church and state and the increased threat of secularity in the church because of the Christianization of the population. Powerful bishops emerged, such as Ambrose of Milan (340–97); Jerome (340–420), the monastic scholar who created the Bible of the Middle Ages, the Latin Vulgate; Chrysostom (345–407), the eloquent preacher and bishop of Constantinople; Eusebius of Caesarea (c. 263–340), the church's first historian; and Cyril of Jerusalem (c. 315–86), an eminent pastor and writer.

The Trinity of God

One of the greatest benefits of the church's new prominence in the empire was that theological discussion could be conducted on a more extensive basis than ever before. Important questions touching the heart of the Christian faith could be resolved with an openness that had not been possible during the era of persecution the church had endured. The triumph of the

A gigantic sculpted head of the Emperor Constantine the Great.

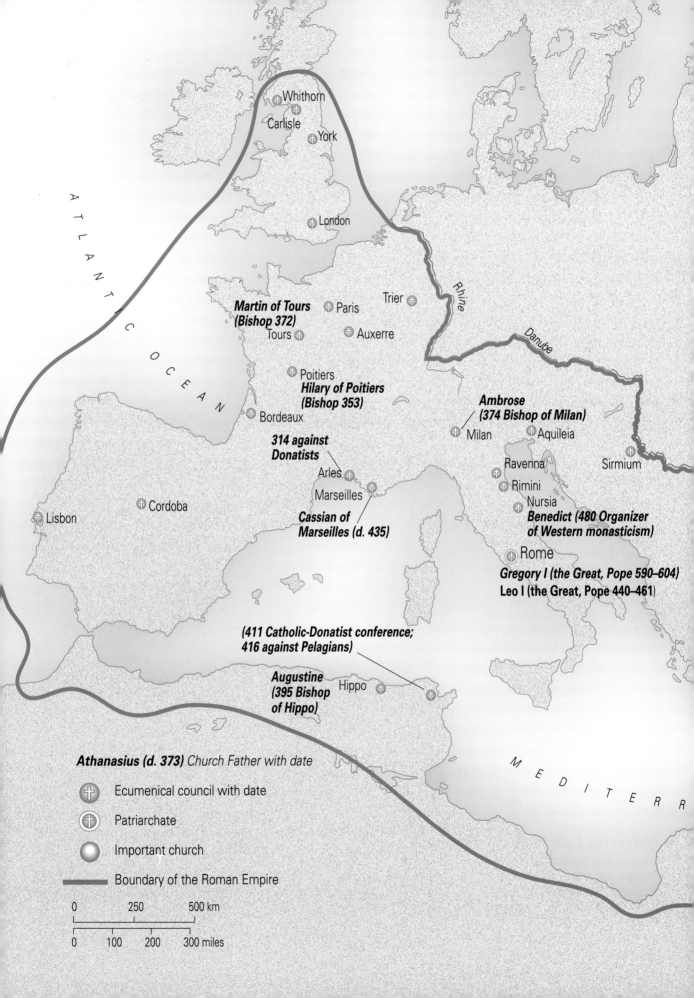

ATLANTIC OCEAN

Whithorn

Carlisle

York

London

Martin of Tours
(Bishop 372)

Paris

Trier

Rhine

Tours

Auxerre

Poitiers

Hilary of Poitiers
(Bishop 353)

Danube

Bordeaux

Ambrose
(374 Bishop of Milan)

Milan

Aquileia

Sirmium

314 against
Donatists

Arles

Ravenna

Marseilles

Rimini

Nursia

Lisbon

Cordoba

Cassian of
Marseilles (d. 435)

Benedict (480 Organizer
of Western monasticism)

Rome

Gregory I (the Great, Pope 590–604)
Leo I (the Great, Pope 440–461)

(411 Catholic-Donatist conference;
416 against Pelagians)

Augustine
(395 Bishop
of Hippo)

Hippo

MEDITERR

Athanasius (d. 373) *Church Father with date*

✠ Ecumenical council with date

✠ Patriarchate

● Important church

━━ Boundary of the Roman Empire

0   250   500 km

0   100   200   300 miles

The Golden Age of the Church Fathers, 4th to 5th Centuries

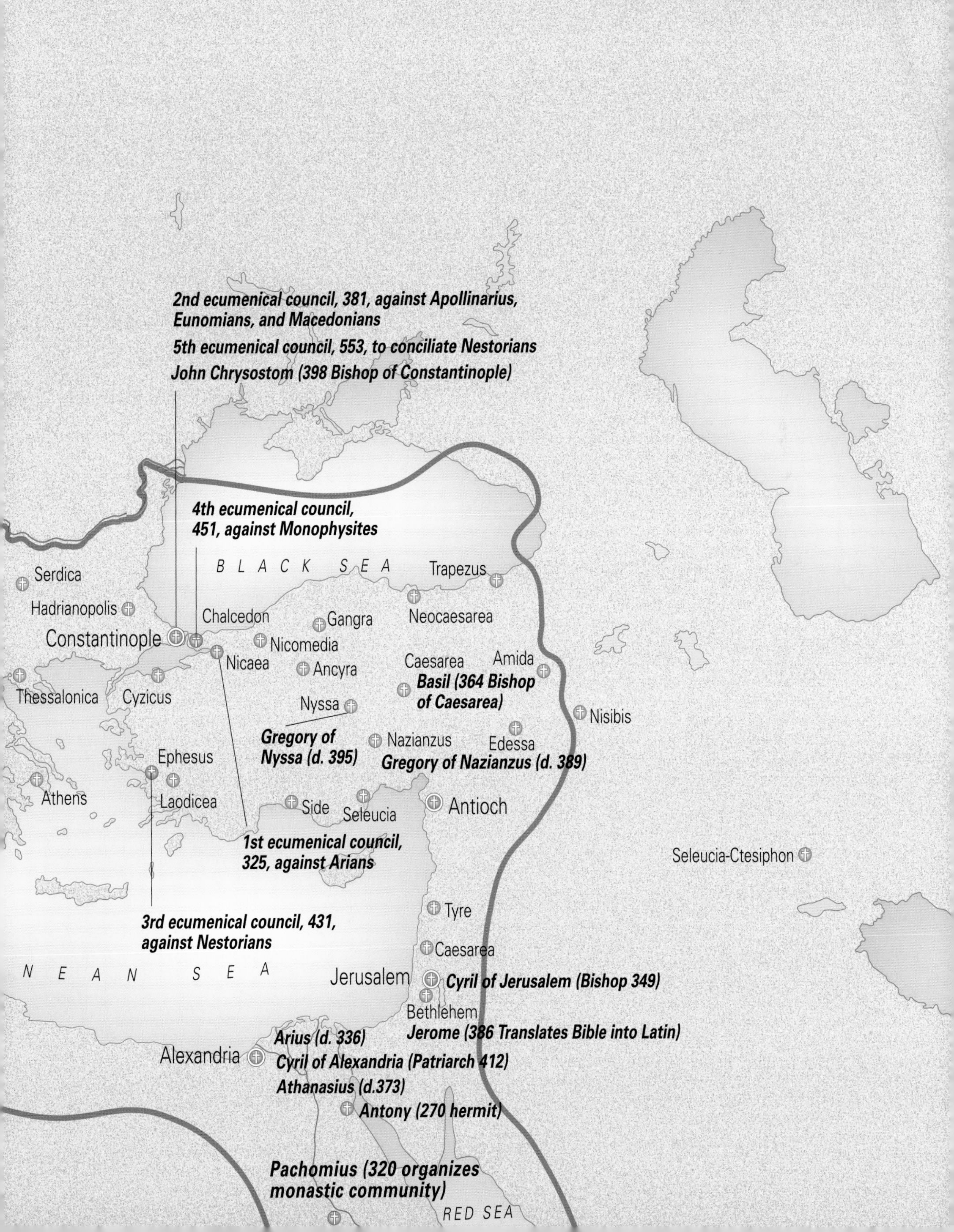

2nd ecumenical council, 381, against Apollinarius, Eunomians, and Macedonians

5th ecumenical council, 553, to conciliate Nestorians

John Chrysostom (398 Bishop of Constantinople)

4th ecumenical council, 451, against Monophysites

BLACK SEA

Serdica

Hadrianopolis

Trapezus

Chalcedon

Gangra

Neocaesarea

Constantinople

Nicomedia

Nicaea

Ancyra

Caesarea

Amida

Basil (364 Bishop of Caesarea)

Thessalonica

Cyzicus

Nyssa

Nisibis

Gregory of Nyssa (d. 395)

Nazianzus

Edessa

Gregory of Nazianzus (d. 389)

Ephesus

Athens

Laodicea

Side

Seleucia

Antioch

1st ecumenical council, 325, against Arians

3rd ecumenical council, 431, against Nestorians

Tyre

NEAN SEA

Caesarea

Jerusalem

Cyril of Jerusalem (Bishop 349)

Bethlehem

Jerome (386 Translates Bible into Latin)

Arius (d. 336)

Alexandria

Cyril of Alexandria (Patriarch 412)

Athanasius (d.373)

Antony (270 hermit)

Seleucia-Ctesiphon

Pachomius (320 organizes monastic community)

RED SEA

Nicene and Post-Nicene Fathers

Name	Dates	Location	Important Works	Important Facts
Eusebius	c. 263–c. 339	Caesarea	Ecclesiastical History Chronicle Life of Constantine	Known as father of church history Friend and advisor of Constantine Bishop of Caesarea Sought compromise in Arian controversy
Athanasius	c. 296–373	Alexandria	On the Incarnation of the Divine Word Against Apollinarius	Most noted defender of Trinitarian orthodoxy Named patriarch of Alexandria in 328 Vocal participant in Council of Nicea Exiled five times Lived ascetic life
Basil	c. 329–379	Cappadocia	Five books against Eunomius	Lived ascetic life Became bishop of Caesarea in Cappadocia Opposed Arianism

church in the Roman Empire was characterized by a succession of great ecumenical councils. Although these councils convened under the auspices of the emperor, they allowed churchmen throughout the empire to gather and discuss whatever was troubling the unity of the churches and bring resolution through the writing of creeds. (These councils and creeds have been called "ecumenical" because they were the gatherings and decisions of the entire church leadership.)

The first issue that troubled the church was that of the relationship of the preincarnate Christ to God the Father. What was Christ before He came to earth? How can the church credibly confess that Jesus is God (its universal proclamation) and yet maintain its belief that God is one? If Christ is not really and completely God, how could He gain for us what He did not possess, the life of God? In retrospect, we can appreciate Tertullian's insight when he spoke of God as "three in one cohering," but his association with the radically critical Montanists caused his contributions to be shunned by many.

Adoptionism

Prior to the fourth century, there were two attempts to explain the relationship of the Father to the Son: adoptionism and modalism. Adoptionists, such as Paul of Samosota, bishop of Antioch, denigrated the equality of the Father–Son relationship when they argued that Christ was an elevated human being, infused at His baptism by superhuman characteristics. The bishop spoke of Christ as one with the Father—but only in power or purpose rather than essential being. Paul of Samosota was condemned in 268 at a regional council in his own city. His view never became a dominating error troubling the churches.

Modalism

Modalism or patripassionism (which suggests the Father suffered on the cross) rent the church more deeply. Advocates such as Praxeas and Sabellius argued that God is one in person, yet three in separate manifestations. According to Praxeas's opponent Tertullian, he taught that "the Father Himself came down in the Virgin, was Himself born of her, Himself suffered, indeed, was Himself Jesus Christ." Modalists were strong advocates of the unity of God, but spoke of that unity in such a way as to deny the diversity of persons in the Godhead.

Arius

The issue of the relationship between Father and Son flared again in the fourth century, but this time Christian issues were of empire-wide importance. Arius (c. 250–336), a presbyter in Alexandria, Egypt, was discovered to be teaching that Christ was not equal with God, but that He was created in eternity. (The Father and Son therefore would not share absolute equality of divine characteristics.) Arius saw the Trinity as a triad of persons, but not in equal glory. From an Arian perspective, the Savior is not God, only a creature. Arius was condemned at a council in Alexandria in 321, his writings were burned, and he was subsequently banished, although he continued to propagate his views through the medium of

An artist's impression of the Council of Nicaea, 325.

song. (The Council of Laodicea [363] reacted by disallowing congregational singing in the churches.)

Council of Nicaea

As discussion over the relationship of the Father and Son continued—often with violence—the emperor sought to resolve the threatening tensions by gathering together the bishops of the church. More than three hundred bishops met at Nicaea, a town near the capital of Constantinople, to settle the issue. However, the bishops were divided. A minority of bishops, following the notions of the modalist Sabellius, contended that the concept of monotheism demanded that Christ be understood as a lesser being than God the Father. The emperor intervened in the discussions and suggested that the way to explain the relationship of the Father to the Son was to think of unity and equality of attributes (essence); this, he felt, secured the doctrine of the deity of Christ. This was expressed in the Nicaean Creed in the words "begotten not made, of one substance with the Father." Many, but not all, felt that the statement tacitly condemned Arianism. Thus concluded the first worldwide gathering of the church's leadership.

The Arian Controversy

However, the controversy did not end with the conclusion of the Nicaean Council, because the terms used in the creed were interpreted variously, particularly the words "of the same substance." Some eastern bishops accused supporters of the creed of advocating modalism, because the phrase "same substance" was used by Sabellius to stress the oneness of God. Nicaea used it from a western viewpoint to signify one of the characteristics in the midst of a plurality of persons. Arian teachings surged in popularity and the empire was threatened with division. Through the work of Basil of Caesarea (d. 379), Gregory of Nazianzus (329–89), and Gregory of Nyssa (d. 395), the terms of the discussion, complicated by the linguistic differences between West and East, were resolved.

Council of Constantinople

Theodosius I, the emperor who declared Christianity as the sole religion of the empire in 380, called another council of the church in the capital, the Council of Constantinople (381). The council affirmed the previous ecumenical council and its findings; the party of the great Athanasius of Alexandria prevailed. The doctrine of the trinity of God was agreeably explained. All the divine attributes were asserted to be equally and fully shared by three distinct persons. The trinity of God should be spoken of as God, the Father; God, the Son; and God, the Holy Spirit. Finally, the church was able to explain its faith.

In the discussion of the relationship of the Father to the Son, the issue of the Holy Spirit emerged as a logical corollary. The focus on the deity of the Savior at Nicaea precluded an emphasis on the Spirit. (The creed simply affirms "and in the Holy Spirit.") Between the two great councils, a group emerged called the Macedonians who took the same view of the Spirit that the Arians did of Christ. They asserted that the Spirit is a creature. However, if the Holy Spirit is the life giver, how can He grant life that He does not possess? At a regional synod in Alexandria in 362, the Macedonians were condemned,

Coin showing Constantine giving his legions the famous Chi-Rho monogram, also known as the labarum.

Ecumenical Councils of the Early Church

Place	Date	Emperor	Major Participants	Significant Result
Nicaea	325	Constantine	Arius Alexander Eusebius of Nicomedia Eusebius of Caesarea Athanasius	Declared Son *homoousios* (coequal, consubstantial, and coeternal) with Father Condemned Arius Drafted original form of Nicene Creed
Constantinople	381	Theodosius I	Apollinarius Gregory of Nazianzus Gregory of Nyssa	Confirmed results of Council of Nicea Produced revised Nicene Creed Ended Trinitarian Controversy Affirmed deity of the Holy Spirit Condemned Apollinarianism
Ephesus	431	Theodosius II	Nestorius Cyril	Declared Nestorianism heretical Condemned Pelagius
Chalcedon	451	Marcian	Eutyches Leo I	Declared Christ's two natures unmixed unchanged, undivided, inseparable Condemned Eutychianism
Constantinople	553	Justinian	Severus of Antioch Julian of Halicarnassus	Affirmed Cyril's interpretation of Chalcedon

paving the way for their greater rejection at Constantinople. The church was able to end the discussion of the trinity of God.

Ironically, the Council of Constantinople was not recognized as a universal council throughout the churches, because no western bishops attended. It was not until the seventh century that it was declared such by Gregory the Great, the first pope in the West. In attempting to assert his authority over the churches, he may have been attracted to the third canon of the council that asserted the primacy of the church of Constantinople after that of Rome.

The Person of Jesus Christ

In the midst of the discussion of the relationship of the Father to the Son, which led to the explication of the trinitarian faith, a question arose about the incarnate Son. What was the relationship of His humanity to His deity? From the earliest period of

Christian thought, the leaders of the church recognized two errors in this regard: the Docetists, who denied Jesus' humanity, making the Incarnation appear as a charade; and the Ebionites, who affirmed Christ's humanity but relegated His deity to moral excellence. In the West, Tertullian referred to Christ as possessing two distinct natures in one person. Many generally followed him, though his associations with the condemned Montanists prevented appreciation of his insights in this regard. Later, Augustine expressed Tertullian's insights and they prevailed in the West.

Apollinarius
In the East, the relationship of the two natures of Christ continued to cause serious controversy. Apollinarius (c. 310–90), bishop of Laodicea and a strong ally of Athanasius of Alexandria, argued that Christ possessed all the attributes of deity, but in a humanity that was incomplete. According to Apollinarius, Christ

was not truly human because He was devoid of a human rational faculty. The bishop was willing to sacrifice His humanity in order to preserve His deity. Churchmen found this view of the incarnate Christ as destructive as Arius's pre-incarnate view of Him; such notions destroyed the central message of the church, namely salvation through Christ. Can one less than God redeem unto God? Can a lesser being satisfy the demands of a greater being if the demands of the greater are His perfections?

Gregory of Nazianzus
Gregory of Nazianzus, one of three great champions of orthodoxy of the era, the Cappodocians, argued "that which He has not assumed He has not healed. If only half [of] Adam fell, then that which Christ assumes is half also; but if the whole of his nature fell, it must be united to the whole nature of Him that was begotten and be saved as a whole." At the Council of

Early illustration of Theodosius I at the Council of Ephesus, 431.

Constantinople in 381, the churchmen that gathered evaluated Apollinarius's view of Christ and condemned it, expressing in the creed that Christ "became human." However the mystery of the Incarnation might be explained, it could not be at the expense of either Christ's deity or His humanity.

Nestorius

The condemnation of Apollinarianism did not end the controversy because the council did not put forth a statement on the issue that was agreeable to the churches. In 428, Nestorius became the bishop of Constantinople and renewed the controversy by asserting that Mary may be said to bear Christ but not God. He affirmed two perfect natures of Christ, but did not seem to affirm the unity of those two persons in one nature. He argued: "My good friend, Mary has not born the Godhead, for that which is flesh is flesh. . . . A creature has not born the creator, but she bore a man, the organ of divinity."

Nestorius was condemned by Cyril, the bishop of Alexandria, in 430. However, John, the bishop of Antioch, supported Nestorius. (The motive for one bishop to take sides against another cannot be divorced from ecclesiastical rivalry and the desire for a superior place among the churches.) The developing chaos caused the emperor to call another general council to resolve the problem. With only a scattering of bishops present at the Council of Ephesus in 431, and most favoring Cyril's view, Nestorius was quickly condemned. When the pro-Nestorian delegation arrived shortly thereafter, they met separately and condemned Cyril. The confrontation was resolved when a delegate from Bishop Celeste of Rome arrived. He sided with the supporters of Cyril and condemned Nestorius and John of Antioch. The precedent of appealing to Rome to adjudicate controversy would prove important for later papal claims to superiority. Celeste was willing to side with Cyril in condemning Nestorius in exchange for his condemnation of a heretic in the West named Pelagius. Greed of place and rivalry figured largely in the discussion. Nestorius and John were both condemned to exile. However Nestorius lived beyond the resolution of the controversy and confessed that the orthodox statement was really what he was trying to express.

Eutyches

When Eutyches (c. 378–454), the head of a monastery in Constantinople, offered a resolution to the continuing crisis, it was brought to a solution—though not in the way he had hoped. Though Eutyches accepted the complete deity and humanity of the Savior in one person, he felt that one person could only imply one nature. He rejected the council's phrase, "two natures after the incarnation," arguing instead that Christ was of one nature, a complex of both, and therefore not one with human beings in His new humanity. In other words, His humanity was absorbed into His deity. Eutyches believed that any affirmation of two distinct natures in Christ was an affirmation of Nestorianism, a condemned heresy. He was condemned by his bishop, Flavian of Constantinople, at a local synod, saying that "I confess that our Lord was of two natures before the union, but after the union [the Incarnation] one nature."

Robbers Synod of Ephesus

The controversy spilled across the

empire when Eutyches claimed support for his views from a previous bishop of Alexandria and appealed to the bishop of Rome, Leo I. The emperor called a council in 449 at Ephesus, which was presided over by Dioscorus, bishop of Alexandria. The decision of the council was determined before it began, however, because of Dioscorus's prejudice against Eutyches for implicating his bishopric in the Nestorian error. Leo sided with Flavian, and the letter he sent, though influential in the final formula, was not presented as evidence at the council. Dioscorus expelled Flavian from the church and he died shortly thereafter. The acrimony expressed at this council is the reason it has been dubbed "the Robbers Synod." The rivalry and radical factions at the council precluded any serious resolution of the issue.

Council of Chalcedon

Within a year, however, the emperor died in an accident and the new emperor, who favored the bishop of Rome, opened the same issue and called for a new council. Five hundred and twenty bishops gathered at Chalcedon, a town near Constantinople, in 451, in what has been designated as the Fourth Ecumenical Council of the church. The influence of Leo's previous letter proved pivotal in resolving the controversy.

Following the insights of Tertullian, Leo argued that Christ was one person consisting of two perfect, distinct natures, one divine and one human. The formulation of the council, *The Definition of Faith*, defined the incarnate Christ as having "two natures, without confusion, without change, without division, without separation." It was Leo who insisted that this had to be the teaching of Scripture because of the church's understanding of redemption. If Christ redeemed His people by paying a debt of infinite magnitude for them, He

Remains of the Church of St. John, Ephesus. After Constantine made Christianity a legal religion, many buildings for Christian worship were constructed.

had to be infinite Himself while also being human. Being God, He could satisfy the infinite demands of divine justice and do so as a human substitute. If the basis of forgiveness is the very satisfaction of the divine character (justice and wrath) and God only accepts that which is in perfect congruity with Himself, then Christ must be God. However, He also had to be a man, because only a human could take the place of humans on the cross.

Thus, the Chalcedonian position of the church, relative to the incarnate Christ, is that He is fully God (100 percent), fully man (100 percent), in one person, without confusion. As John 1:14 aptly states: "The Word [Christ] became flesh [human] and tabernacled [a symbol of God's presence among his ancient people] among us."

Mary As "Mother of God"

The twenty-eighth canon of the Chalcedonian Council redefined the third canon of the Constantinople Council (381), stating that the phrase "Constantinople was first after Rome" meant that as bishoprics they were equal in authority and

prestige. The rivalry of the bishops is a persistent theme in the early centuries of the church. Also, the Chalcedonian *Definition of Faith* refers to Mary as the mother of God, a strange phrase to modern Protestants because of the later usage of it by the Medieval Catholic Church. It was Cyril who introduced this phrase into the Nestorian Controversy. (Nestorius argued that Mary bore only the man Jesus, not God in her womb, thus seemingly dividing Christ into two persons.) The point of the words "mother of God" is that Mary gave birth to more than a human being. In a divine mystery beyond explanation, she bore in her womb the Creator and Redeemer of the universe. She is not equal with God or superior in any way to other women, but she was graciously given a unique privilege.

Council of Contantinople

Though Eutychianism (single nature Christology) was condemned at a worldwide gathering of the church's leadership, segments of the church chafed over the findings of Chalcedon. How can there be two

Pope Leo I, "Leo the Great," d. 461.

distinct sets of qualities in one person, given that a person is a single set of qualities? Later known as Monophysitism, this view was condemned at another ecumenical council, the Council of Constantinople (553). The second condemnation by the church of this view of Christ caused the first major division of the church that continues to the present day. The Western churches and the Orthodox Church (the result of a later schism in the Chalcedonian churches) follow Chalcedon and dual-nature explanations of the incarnate Christ. The churches of Ethiopia and Egypt, the Marionites, and the Armenians are examples of those who believe that the incarnate Christ is best conceived as having had one nature.

The Contribution of Augustine

The most influential churchman of the era—and arguably in the history of the church—was Augustine of North Africa (354–430), bishop of Hippo. Raised in the home of a pagan father and a saintly mother, Monica, he studied rhetoric in Carthage and eventually went to Rome to pursue a career. Immoral in lifestyle and a religious profligate, he experienced a life-changing conversion and was baptized by Ambrose, bishop of Milan, in 387. Returning to Africa, Augustine entered a monastery where he thought he could best serve his new Lord. In 391, he was ordained a priest, and five years later his piety and giftedness was recognized in his appointment as bishop of Hippo. He continued in that office until he died in his home city at the age of eighty-six.

Augustine became a prolific defender of the faith. He initially wrote against the Manichees—a Gnostic sect that had attracted him as a youth—and also debated the Donatists, a separatist sect. He is best known for his writings against Pelagius, a monk from Britain. Each of these controversies shaped Augustine's explanation of the faith, and his explanation in turn shaped the teachings of the church for centuries.

Augustine's writings

Several of his writings have become classics. In 400, he completed his *Confessions*, the first spiritual autobiography in the history of the church written in the first person and addressed to God. Often quoted is his memorable line from the first page of the book: "The heart of man is restless until it finds its rest in you." *The City of God,* a work begun in 413 and completed in 426, was of monumental significance in the shaping of the Christian community. In this treatise, Augustine sought to explain why the Roman Empire, having become Christian, was rapidly disintegrating. Was it the fault of the Christians? In what amounted to the first Christian interpretation of history, Augustine explained why nations rise and fall. History is not a repetitive cycle without progress; it is a divinely inspired redemptive drama: the story of two cities formed by two loves. The city of man—formed by self-love—is the world; the city of God—formed by love of God—is the redeemed. These two cities exist together in time, but at the end they will be separated. The city of man will endure eternal condemnation; the city of God an eternity of bliss in the presence of God.

Augustine and Grace

Augustine's controversy with the Donatists shaped his ideas of the church, and his influence stretched for centuries. His opponents argued that the benefit the church possesses and dispenses is dependent upon the holiness of its officers and members. Augustine, however, argued that the grace of God is not dependent on the qualities of the minister, but upon the wonder of God's grace. And because God's grace comes through the church, it is crucial that one be a member of the Catholic Church, the one universal church. Augustine quipped, "There is a great difference between an apostle and a drunkard; but there is no difference at all between a Christian baptism performed by a drunkard. . . . There is no difference between a Christian baptism performed by an apostle and that performed by a heretic." The church, being the repository of grace from God, is the means of the distribution of grace to people. The church is the redeeming community, and there is no salvation outside of it. A heretic or immoral person in the church authentically conveys grace through his official functions.

Augustine and Baptism

Other important contributions of Augustine's teachings that shaped subsequent centuries were his ideas about baptism and justifying grace. No evidence exists in the second century that those incapable of learning were the subjects of baptism. (The term *infant* is used in the literature, but the term is not age specific.) However, baptism of infants did gradually become a practice in the churches, particularly after the dominance of the church in the empire. Newborn infants were admitted to the state by birth and to the church (the saved community) through baptism.

Baptism was believed to remove the stain of original sin, the guilt of Adamic union. The effect of baptism was to destroy inability and leave people with only personal sins (called concupiscence). Evil is the absence of righteousness; it is a defect, not an effect. Formal entrance into the church came through confirmation, a practice that became common about the same time. Further, Augustine understood the idea of justification, a right standing before God, to be the result of a process of progressive religious improvement that culminates in glorification. (He was not aware of declarative, once-for-all-time imputed righteousness.) Sins left unconfessed at death would be removed in purgatory, another doctrine he championed in the church. His doctrine of redemption was that of gradual purgation, not a definitive forgiveness through divine declaration.

The Augustinian–Pelagian Controversy

At the close of the fourth century, Pelagius—a monk from Britain—came to Rome, where he became an influential teacher. His writings came to the attention of Augustine and occasioned a controversy that continues today. To what degree has the sin of Adam affected the human race? Can a human being by self-effort or assisted effort come to God? Pelagius believed that the way to preserve the integrity of the moral responsibility affirmed in the Bible, and to defend the church against

The interior of St. Peter's basilica, Rome, built by Constantine the Great.

the charge of fatalism (the idea that human actions are not real), was to assume every person's ability to come to God of his own natural ability. In other words, people have the ability to please God so as to necessitate His kindness in return. A horrified Augustine argued that Adam's sin left humanity in a state of gracelessness and corruption from birth. Citing Romans 5:12, he commented, "And thus 'by one man sin entered into the world, and death by sin, and so death passed upon all men for that all have sinned.' By the 'world' the apostle, of course, means in this place the whole human race."

Free Will
Pelagius went on to define free will as a natural ability possessed by all to determine their moral and religious destinies. Augustine opposed any notion that the grace of God could be dispensed because of human efforts. He argued that freedom of the will is the ability to act according to the dictates of one's pleasures and dislikes; the will is free to act in conformity to its nature. Therefore, because man's nature is absolutely corrupted and incapable of any good before God, he *is* free, but

only to be gladly lost forever. The basis of God's favor cannot be rooted in the stumbling creature but in God alone, argued Augustine. The cause of the creature's redemption is God's unmerited and uncaused favor. That favor is distributed in a discriminatory fashion based on God's mere choice. "This grace is, however, of Christ. Without which neither infants nor adults can be saved, is not rendered for any merits, but is given *gratis*, on account of which it is also called *grace.*"

Foreknowledge
To explain why some embrace Christ and others do not, Augustine believed that the answer is not in human ability to impress or reject God, as Pelagius taught, but in God alone. In eternity past, God chose to redeem some from lost humanity by appointing or predestining them to life. The basis of His choice was His foreknowledge. "Foreknowledge" is not God's awareness of what a creature may or may not do at some future time if the gospel was preached to him (as if the final choice rested in the creature), but is God's timeless redeeming love for the creature.

Predestination

To Augustine, foreknowledge does not mean prior knowledge but prior love. The meriting of salvation is the work of Christ alone, based upon God's determination to be gracious, not at all upon creaturely insight. The key to Augustine's system is unmerited grace through predestination; the key to Pelagius's system is human ability. Augustine found the only hope for redemption in God, whereas Pelagius found it in the ability of the creature to move God. In Pelagius's view, the creature has something that he has not been given—and therefore has grounds for boasting in his salvation. Augustine's view is that of a helpless sinner who is completely rescued from his merited plight by the unmerited, uncaused mercies of God. "God's predestination of good is, as I have said, the preparation of grace; which grace is the effect of that predestination."

Council of Ephesus

Pelagius's views were condemned at the ecumenical Council of Ephesus in 431. The rejection of the Pelagian perspective was the result of a compromise reached between influential bishops. Eastern bishops were struggling against the views of Nestorius; the Western bishops against Pelagius. Further, in condemning Pelagius, many bishops in the West were troubled by the implications of Augustine's insistence on predestinarianism. At this time, churches in northwest Africa were crushed by the invading tribes that rampaged the empire, adding immense social uncertainty and disruption.

John Cassian

The loss to the Christian faith of North Africa resulted in a new intellectual center of the western church: Gaul (France). In these troubling times, John Cassian, a monastic, sought to compromise the harshness of Augustine's views.

He argued that sin was a serious problem for mankind, disagreeing with Pelagius, but contended it was not as totally debilitating as Augustine taught. The effect of sin was more of a weakness than a death, and the creature has some measure of ability.

Cassian's notion seems to have been that of a causative cooperative ability; God is most gracious, but some merit for salvation is found in a sincere willingness to believe the gospel. He rejected the notion of unconditional election and defined foreknowledge as foreseen faith. According to Cassian, those who perish do so against God's will. The controversy continued in the Western churches and occasioned a gathering of the leadership to resolve it: the Synod of Orange in 529.

Synod of Orange

The synod condemned both the teachings of Pelagius that salvation is based on human ability and Cassian's view of a cooperation between God and man, each contributing what the other does not. The third canon states, "Whoever says that the grace of God can be bestowed in reply to human petition (that ability precedes grace), but not that the grace brings it about so that it is asked for by us (grace precedes ability), contradicts Isaiah the prophet and the Apostle (Isa. 65:1; Rom. 10:20)."

The synod affirmed an essential Augustinianism (human inability,

Medieval depiction of Augustine of Hippo.

Statue of Jerome at Bethlehem, where he settled as leader of the monastery.

The ancient monastery of St. Catherine's lies isolated in the Sinai desert, Egypt.

unmerited grace) that prevailed into the Medieval Period, though by neglect the church did not embrace Augustine's predestinarianism. Without this doctrine, Augustine had argued, his teachings on the uncaused favor of God lacked a rational explanation. If a person is redeemed, it is because of God's unmerited mercies in Christ, not by anything in the creature, even in the slightest, lest he have a basis for boasting.

In subsequent centuries, the stigma of Augustinian harshness led many to redefine the doctrine of predestination and to soften the doctrine of human inability. The keystone of the gospel story from the human viewpoint is human inability and condemnation that necessitates the unmerited mercies of the divine Redeemer. From a divine point of view, the keystone is God's electing mercy that absolutely assures the salvation of anyone whom God savingly draws to Himself.

The Rise of Monasticism

Monasticism, which rose in the late third and fourth centuries, emerged from the genuine desire of many to follow the Lord in separation from the world. In the earliest centuries, sincere Christian discipleship was expressed in martyrdom. With the change of the church's status in the empire in the fourth century, following Christ found expression in a new form of sacrificial expression. To the monk, separation from the world and its pleasures was not a way of escape or of somehow pleasing God; it was a means of putting the Bible into practice in the cultivation of non-worldly virtues. Silence reined in a loose, deceitful tongue; manual labor countered slothfulness; trust for the necessities of life overcame materialism and greed. Buffeting the body and limiting the satisfaction of its desires seemed a wonderful way to express Christian devotion. (However, there was a dark side to this form of Christian spirituality.)

Antony of Egypt
The earliest forms of monasticism arose in Egypt in the hermitic practices: individuals living isolated in caves. Antony of Egypt (d. 356) was celebrated as the ideal of piety in Athanasius's biography of him, which contributed significantly to the movement's popularity. Another well-known, even bizarre, manifestation of isolationist godliness was Simon Stylites, who sat on columns of various heights above the earth for years praying, counseling, and preaching.

Pachomius
Not all monks chose the path of isolation. In the fourth century, communities of Christ-followers emerged. These can be traced back to Pachomius (292–346), a hermit who established a large community of monks on an island in the Nile River. Monks slept several to a cell, ate in common, practiced strict silence, engaged in manual labor, and practiced the disciplines of prayer and Bible reading. Monasticism also spread rapidly in the East through such prominent churchmen as Basil of Caesarea and Chrysostom. The monasteries stressed the need for social and religious service.

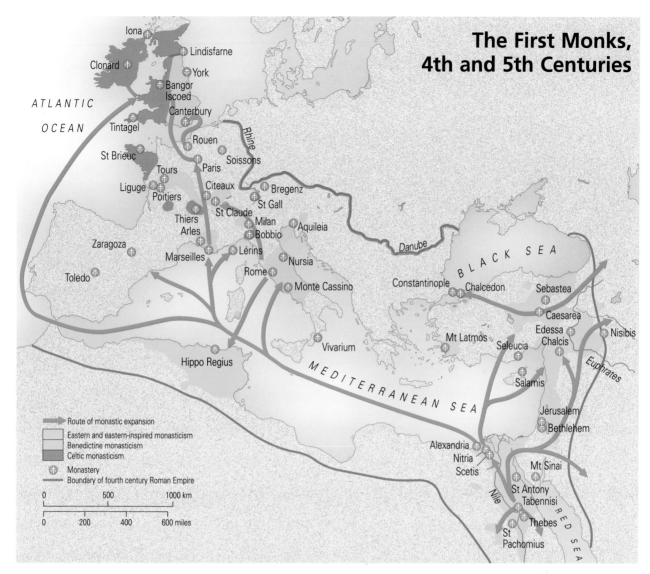

The First Monks,
4th and 5th Centuries

Iona
Lindisfarne
Clonard
York
Bangor
Iscoed
Canterbury
ATLANTIC
OCEAN
Tintagel
Rouen
Rhine
St Brieuc
Soissons
Tours
Paris
Liguge
Citeaux
Bregenz
Poitiers
St Gall
Thiers
St Claude
Milan
Arles
Bobbio
Aquileia
Zaragoza
Lérins
Marseilles
Nursia
Toledo
Rome
Monte Cassino
Constantinople
Chalcedon
Sebastea
BLACK SEA
Caesarea
Edessa
Nisibis
Chalcis
Mt Latmos
Seleucia
Euphrates
Vivarium
Hippo Regius
Salamis
MEDITERRANEAN SEA
Jerusalem
Bethlehem
Danube
Alexandria
Nitria
Mt Sinai
Scetis
Nile
St Antony
Tabennisi
RED SEA
Thebes
St
Pachomius

Route of monastic expansion
Eastern and eastern-inspired monasticism
Benedictine monasticism
Celtic monasticism
Monastery
Boundary of fourth century Roman Empire

0   500   1000 km
0   200   400   600 miles

Education, hospitality, and health care were a constant part of the contemplative life of the monk.

Benedict of Nursia
Western monasticism was introduced by Athanasius and popularized by Ambrose, Jerome, Augustine, Martin of Tours, and John Cassian. The monastic ideal was stated by Benedict of Nursia (480–543). He established a string of self-sufficient monasteries beginning with Monte Cassino, Italy, in 529, but regulated them with his famous *Vow* or *Rule*. Though not entirely original, Benedict's *Rule* emphasized the authority of the abbot in the monastery, communal worship, manual labor, Bible reading, and charity. By the time of

Charlemagne in the ninth century, the monastic ideal was universal within Christendom.

Early Missions
The record of the expansion of the faith is tantalizingly meager. The book of Acts provides some valuable information about the church's growth from its initial beginnings to its spread to the capital of the empire, Rome. We know that the most potent influences in the spread of the faith were the family, personal witness, and the gathering of Christians for worship. Their transformed manner of living and vocal witness inspired many others to embrace Christ. So pervasive was the Christian movement, in

spite of severe repression, that the empire embraced it as the religion of the state in the fourth century.

Tribalization of Europe
The triumph of Christianity in the Roman Empire happened at the same time that the empire—which stretched from North Africa to the British Isles and from the Atlantic Ocean to Syria—was threatened from attacks on its frontiers. In Europe, the border of "civilization" was west of the Rhine and south of the Danube. As the Romans were increasingly unable to defend their far-flung borders, the empire began to shrink. The tribalization of Europe began with the defeat of a Roman army at Adrianople in 378. Vandals routed the Romans from

The Church in the West in the 6th Century

CELTS

ANGLES
AND
SAXONS

Iona
Lindisfarne
Armagh
Bangor
York
Canterbury

NORTH

SEA

ATLANTIC

OCEAN

Tournai
Cologne
Rouen
Rheims
Trier
Seine
Rhine
Orleans
Loire
Sens
Nantes
Bourges
Tours
Besançon
Poitiers
KINGDOM
OF THE
FRANKS
Lyons
Rhone
Bordeaux
Clermont
Vienne
Eauze
Embrun
Milan
Aquileia
Toulouse
Orange
Narbonne
Genoa
Ravenna
Braga
Arles
Pisa
Arezzo
Agde
Marseilles
Zaragoza
Tagus
KINGDOM
OF THE
VISIGOTHS
Toledo
Rome
KINGDOM
OF THE
LOMBARDS
Merida
Valencia
Seville
Danube
BYZANTINE EMPIRE
Vivarium

BYZANTINE EMPIRE
Carthage

M E D I T E R R A N E A N   S E

Legend

 Metropolitanate
✝ Bishopric founded before AD 500
✝ Bishopric founded in sixth century
— Boundary of Kingdom

0   250   500 km

0   100   200   300 miles

Conversion of the Barbarians

Tribe	Date of Christianization	Main Missionary/Ruler(s)
Goths	c. 340	Ulfilas (*Arian*)
	c. 720	Boniface (Wynfrith) (*Catholic*)
Burgundians	c. 360	Martin of Tours
Picts	c. 400	Ninian
Irish	c. 435	Patrick
Franks	c. 496	Gregory of Tours/Clovis and Clotilda
Scots	c. 563	Columba
Angles and Saxons	c. 600	Augustine of Canterbury/Ethelbert
Frisians	c. 690	Willibrord

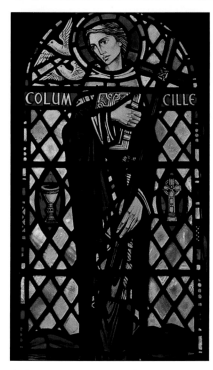

Stained glass depiction of Columba, founder of the monastery at Iona, Scotland.

Boniface (Wynfrith), "Apostle to the Germans" (c. 675–754).

North Africa and sacked Rome in 455. Ostrogoths ruled northern Italy; Visigoths sacked Rome in 410 and settled in Spain; and the Franks settled in Gaul, conquering the Burgundians. By the sixth century, the western Roman Empire was no more.

Christianity and Tribes

The Christian community faced its missionary task out of political and religious necessity. The earliest efforts to Christianize the Germanic tribes came from Arians. Ulfilas (311–83) labored among the Visigoths, converting their language to writing and translating the Scriptures. Martin of Tours (316–96) preached to the Burgundians. In 496, Clovis, the king of the Franks, and his wife, Clotilda, converted to Chalcedonian Christianity through the work of Gregory of Tours. This marked the end of Arian influence among the tribes. As the Franks became dominant, they established a new empire, replacing the old empire of Rome. As a result, the Christian faith triumphed even more.

St. Patrick

A truly remarkable story of early missions to the tribes was the work of St. Patrick of Ireland (389–461). Captured as a youth in Britain as the Roman Empire on that island fell to the Angles, Saxons, and Jutes, Patrick was taken to Ireland as a slave sheep herder. After escaping, he was filled with passion to return to his captors and share with them the Christian faith. His successes are legendary, if not apocryphal (for example, the story of the shamrock). From Ireland, Patrick sent out missionaries to establish monasteries in Ireland, England, and even into Europe to spread the gospel.

Anticipation of the Middle Ages

Out of the ashes of the Roman Empire, the church arose to dominate Europe in an unparalleled era of Christian triumph. Bishops of Rome, excited by new possibilities to extend the Christian faith from their ancient church, became increasingly powerful in state and church affairs. Thus, the stage was set for the Medieval Period, the time between the fall of the Roman Empire and the flowering of the marvelous Renaissance. It was a millennium of triumph and change—but that story awaits our next volume in this series.

Index